CAMBRIDGE PRIMARY
Mathematics

Learner's Book

2

Cherri Moseley and Janet Rees

CAMBRIDGE
UNIVERSITY PRESS

CAMBRIDGE
UNIVERSITY PRESS

University Printing House, Cambridge CB2 8BS, United Kingdom

Cambridge University Press is part of the University of Cambridge.

It furthers the University's mission by disseminating knowledge in the pursuit of education, learning and research at the highest international levels of excellence.

www.cambridge.org
Information on this title: www.cambridge.org/9781107615823

First published 2014

Printed in India by Replika Press Pvt. Ltd

A catalogue record for this publication is available from the British Library

ISBN 978-1-107-61582-3 Paperback

Cover artwork: Bill Bolton

Introduction

This Learner's Book is a supplementary resource that consolidates and reinforces mathematical learning alongside the *Cambridge Primary Mathematics Teacher's Resource 2* (9781107640733). It acts as a useful consolidation tool for the learners by providing points for discussion to develop problem-solving skills and support learning through discovery and discussion. Rote learning and drill exercises are avoided.

Ideally, a session should first be taught using the appropriate *Core activity* in the *Teacher's Resource 2*, and then the *Learner's Book* page is used at the end of the session, or set as homework, as a means of formative assessment. There is a single page corresponding to each *Core activity* in the *Teacher's Resource 2* printed book. The *Core activity* that the page relates to is indicated at the bottom of the page.

Hints and tips are provided throughout to support the learners. They will appear as follows:

Write a list of number pairs to help you

Please note that the *Learner's Book* on its own does not cover all of the Cambridge Primary mathematics curriculum framework for Stage 2. It needs to be used in conjunction with the *Teacher's Resource 2*.

This publication is part of the *Cambridge Primary Maths project*. *Cambridge Primary Maths* is an innovative combination of curriculum and resources designed to support teachers and learners to succeed in primary mathematics through best-practice international maths teaching and a problem-solving approach.

Cambridge Primary Maths brings together the world-class Cambridge Primary mathematics curriculum from Cambridge International Examinations, high-quality publishing from Cambridge University Press and expertise in engaging online enrichment materials for the mathematics curriculum from NRICH.

Teachers have access to an online tool that maps resources and links to materials offered through the primary mathematics curriculum, NRICH and Cambridge Primary mathematics textbooks and e-books. These resources include engaging online activities, best-practice guidance and examples of *Cambridge Primary Maths* in action.

The Cambridge curriculum is dedicated to helping schools develop learners who are confident, responsible, reflective, innovative and engaged. It is designed to give learners the skills to problem solve effectively, apply mathematical knowledge and develop a holistic understanding of the subject.

The *Cambridge Primary Maths* textbooks provide best-in-class support for this problem-solving approach, based on pedagogical practice found in successful schools across the world. The engaging NRICH online resources help develop mathematical thinking and problem-solving skills. To get involved visit www.cie.org.uk/cambridgeprimarymaths

The benefits of being part of *Cambridge Primary Maths* are:
- the opportunity to explore a maths curriculum founded on the values of the University of Cambridge and best practice in schools
- access to an innovative package of online and print resources that can help bring the Cambridge Primary mathematics curriculum to life in the classroom.

This series is arranged to ensure that the curriculum is covered whilst allowing teachers to use a flexible approach. The Scheme of Work for Stage 2 has been followed, though there are a few deviations. The components are:
- Teacher's Resource 2 ISBN: 9781107640733 (printed book and CD-ROM).
- Learner's Book 2 ISBN: 9781107615823 (printed book)
- Games Book 2 ISBN: 9781107623491 (printed book and CD-ROM).

Broken 100 square

Colour these numbers in on your 100 square.

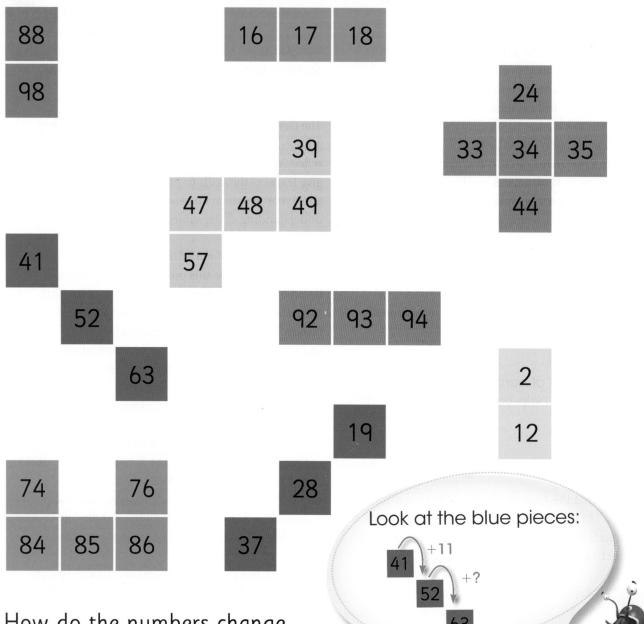

How do the numbers change
as you move up or down each shape?

Choose some squares on your 100 square to shade in a
different colour.
Challenge your partner to describe the pattern you used.

Between decades

Write the numbers between each of the two multiples of 10.

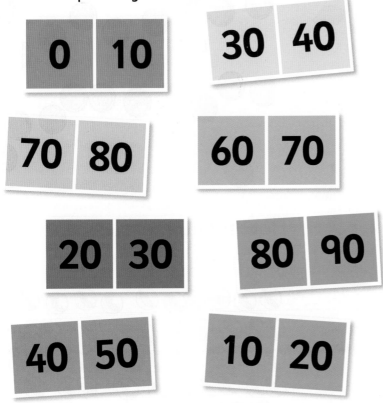

0	**10**

30	**40**

70	**80**

60	**70**

20	**30**

80	**90**

40	**50**

10	**20**

Vocabulary

multiple of 10:
10, 20, 30, 40, 50, 60, 70, 80, 90, 100, 110, 120...
and so on.
They are also known as **decade numbers**.

decade: is ten numbers beginning with a decade number. For example 20, 21, 22, 23, 24, 25, 26, 27, 28 and 29.

midpoint: in an ordered list of numbers, it is the middle number. For example, 5 is the midpoint in the list 1, 2, 3, 4, **5**, 6, 7, 8, 9.

Circle the midpoint of each set of numbers you have written.

Which decades have you not had to write? Write out the decades and find the midpoint.

Decade numbers from 1 to 100:

10	20	30	40	50	60	70	80	90	100

Write the multiples of 10 that each set of numbers is between.

?	**?**

How many?

Count how many shells there are.

How many counters are there?

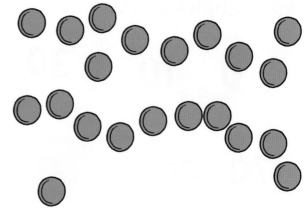

How many marbles can you find?

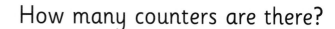

Use a 100 square to help you.

Count the number of beads.

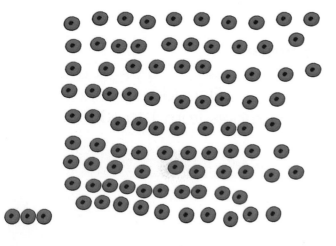

1	2	3	4	5	6	7	8	9	10
11	12	13	14	15	16	17	18	19	20
21	22	23	24	25	26	27	28	29	30
31	32	33	34	35	36	37	38	39	40
41	42	43	44	45	46	47	48	49	50
51	52	53	54	55	56	57	58	59	60
61	62	63	64	65	66	67	68	69	70
71	72	73	74	75	76	77	78	79	80
81	82	83	84	85	86	87	88	89	90
91	92	93	94	95	96	97	98	99	100

Draw 34, 62 and 87 of something.

Group your items in a way that makes them easier to count.

Bags

How many items could be in each bag?

Between 60 and 70

Between 80 and 90

Between 95 and 100

Between 70 and 80

Use a 100 square to help you.

1	2	3	4	5	6	7	8	9	10
11	12	13	14	15	16	17	18	19	20
21	22	23	24	25	26	27	28	29	30
31	32	33	34	35	36	37	38	39	40
41	42	43	44	45	46	47	48	49	50
51	52	53	54	55	56	57	58	59	60
61	62	63	64	65	66	67	68	69	70
71	72	73	74	75	76	77	78	79	80
81	82	83	84	85	86	87	88	89	90
91	92	93	94	95	96	97	98	99	100

More than 40
Less than 60

Less than 80
More than 70

Between 50 and 70

Draw some bags with labels for a partner.

Ask them to tell you how many could be in the bag.

100 grams

A cook put two weights in the pan to check the pan scales were working properly. Which weights could be in the pan?

Vocabulary

Weight: how heavy or light something is.

Weights	
10g	20g
30g	40g
50g	60g
70g	80g
90g	100g

Use pairs of multiples of 10 that make 100 to help you.

Which weights **cannot** be in the pan?

Triangle fact families

Each triangle shows a fact family for number pairs to 100. Copy the triangles and fill in the hidden number on each one.

Vocabulary

fact family: a group of numbers that are related by addition and subtraction facts. For example,

$20 + 80 = 100$

$80 + 20 = 100$

$100 - 20 = 80$

$100 - 80 = 20$

is a fact family.

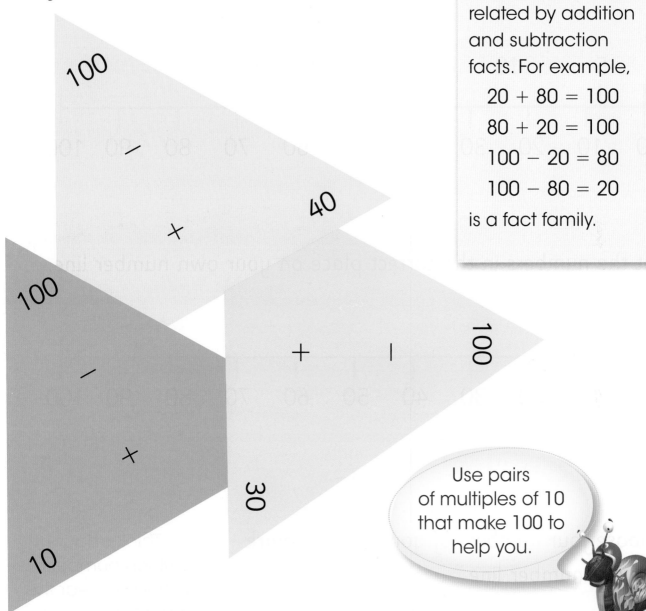

Use pairs of multiples of 10 that make 100 to help you.

Three triangle fact families for 100 are missing. Can you draw them?

Make some triangle fact families for number pairs to 20.

Number line muddle

Some of the numbers on this number line have been marked in the wrong place.

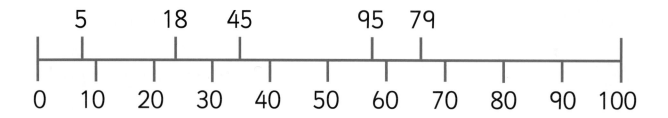

Put the numbers in the correct place on your own number line.

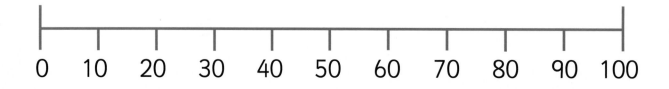

Choose four numbers of your own to mark on your number line.

You could extend your number line to 200 or beyond before marking on your own numbers.

Think about which numbers should be near the numbers you are marking on the number line.

Number drop

Round each number to the nearest 10.

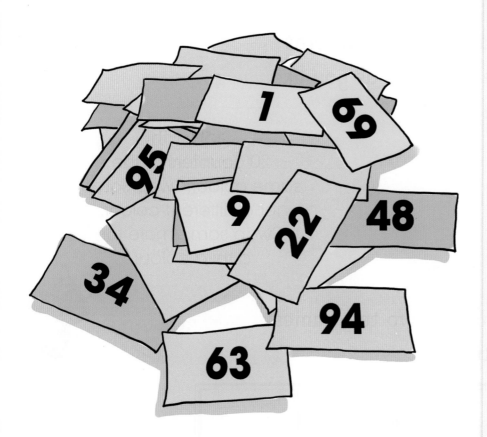

Vocabulary

rounding: rounding to the nearest 10 means giving the closest tens number. Numbers ending in less than 5 are rounded down. Numbers ending in 5 or more are rounded up. For example, 53 rounds to 50; 67 rounds to 70.

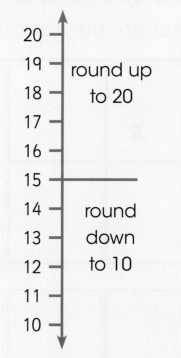

Which two multiples of 10 are left?

For each of those multiples of 10, write a number that would be rounded to it.

Why do you think everyone decided that numbers that end in a 5 should be rounded up?

Twenty

Use counters, cubes or other counting objects to explore 20.

You could add, subtract or make patterns
using as many different colours as you like.
You might have some other
ideas of your own.

Start with
20 counters of the
same colour. Swap some
for a different colour.
Swap some more for
a third colour.

Make up a game using the two ten frames.
What are the instructions?

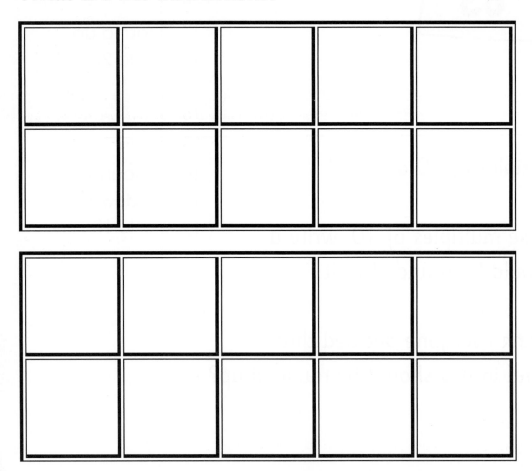

Clock pairs

Draw a large clock face. Here are some examples.

Next to each number on your clock face, write the number pair to 12.

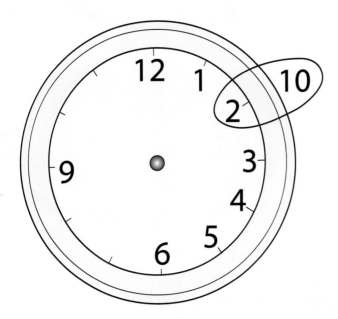

Get 12 counters of one colour and 12 of another colour. Lay them out like a ten frame with two more squares. Swap one counter at a time for the other colour to help you find the number pairs to 12.

Describe the pattern of the numbers you wrote on the clock.

Draw a fact family triangle for two of the number pairs to 12.

Write out the four number facts for each number pair.

How many ways?

There are four sets of numbers below.
Add up the numbers in each set.

Look for pairs to 10, doubles, near doubles, use a number line or try something else.

Now use a different way to add the numbers together.

Remember that you should always get the same total for each set.

Roll a dice to find a new number to add to **one** of the number sets.
Does this change how you add the numbers in that set together?

Hearts and stars

Each card shows one number of a number pair.
The ♥ cards are number pairs to 20.
What number is on the other side of each ♥ card?
Which cards are missing?

Write a list of number pairs to help you.

The ⭐ cards are number pairs to 30.
What number is on the other side of each ⭐ card?
Which cards are missing?

What is the same about each set?
What is different about each set?

Equal machine

The equal machine makes equivalent calculations.

Vocabulary

equal/equivalent: have the same value or amount.

For example, '5 + 2' and '9 − 2' have the same value of 7, so they are equal. They are called equivalent.

Choose a card to go into the equal machine.
What might come out?

36 − 7

11 + 5   23 + 4   22 + 9   39 + 3   9 + 5

13 + 6   17 − 8

What is the longest string of calculations you can make?

Find the value of your chosen card first. Then find lots of ways of making that value.

Arrays

Draw and label these arrays.

array: objects organised into rows and columns so that we can count the objects more easily. For example,

A

B

C

D

2×3
or $3 + 3$
or $2 + 2 + 2$
and so on.

E

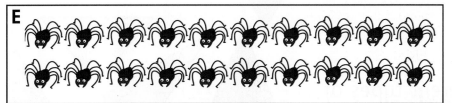

F

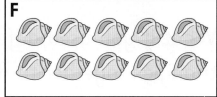

Draw and label some arrays of your own.

How many wheels are there on four tricycles?

A tricycle has three wheels.

If Lucy is paid \$1 for every wheel she cleans, how many dollars does she get to clean five tricycles?

Write a number story about **bicycle** wheel that requires you to calculate an amount in dollars.
Draw an array to solve it.

Shapes

You will need lots of triangles.

Make a **star** shape with some triangles.
How many different star shapes can you make?

How about this one?

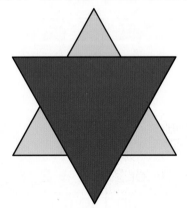

Or this one?

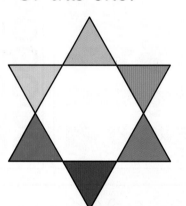

What other shapes can you make?

What if you used different types of triangles together to make a star?

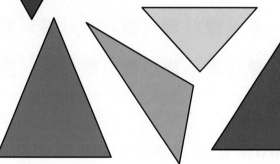

Can you use different shapes to make patterns or pictures?
Can you make shapes with 7, 8 or more sides?
Can you make a pattern or picture with a line of symmetry?

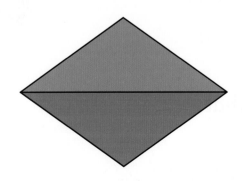
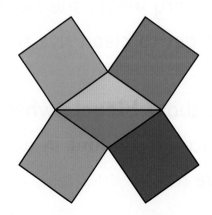

Look for faces

Work with a partner.
You need three cubes all the same size.

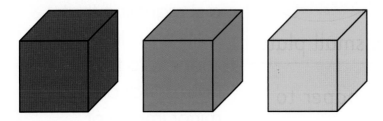

Place one of the cubes in front of you.
You cannot pick up the cube or move it.
How many faces can you see?
Draw the cube and write down next
to your drawing how many faces you can see.

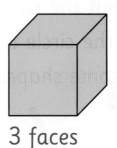

3 faces

Now do the same with two cubes. Put them together
in as many different ways as you can find.
Write down how many faces you can see.

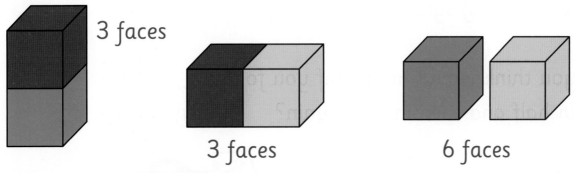

3 faces

3 faces

6 faces

Now do it with three cubes.
Which way can you see the most faces?

What if you use other 3D shapes?
Choose a different shape and see what you can find out.

Paper flowers

You will need:

 A sheet of paper |  Scissors | 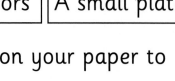 A small plate

1 Draw round the plate on your paper to make a circle.

2 Cut out the circle.

3 Fold the circle in half.

4 Cut some shapes from the folded circle.

 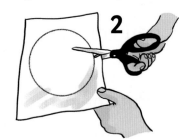 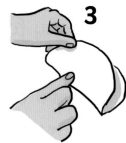 

Open the circle out. What do you notice?
Can you see a line of symmetry?

What do you think would happen if you folded the circle in half and then in half again?

Cut some shapes from the folded circle.

Open the circle.
What do you see? How many **lines of symmetry** can you see now?
What if you folded it three times?

Symmetry

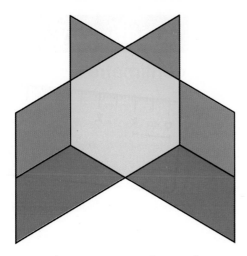

Choose some shapes and make a pattern or picture with one line of symmetry.

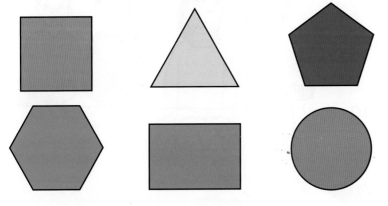

You can make your line of symmetry like this. ———

Or like this. |

Or like this. /

Can you join your symmetrical picture with your partner's symmetrical picture to make a really big picture with one line of symmetry?

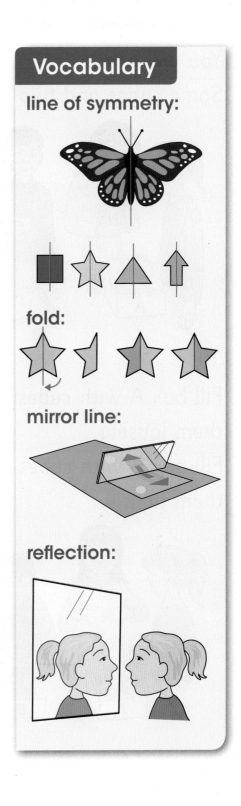

Vocabulary

line of symmetry:

fold:

mirror line:

reflection:

Best box?

You will need:
Some cubes and two boxes.

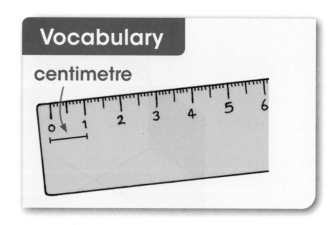

Vocabulary

centimetre

Fill box A with cubes by packing them loosely.
Fill box B with cubes by packing them tightly.

Which box had the most cubes in it? How do you know?

What if you used marbles instead of cubes?
What do you think will happen then?
What do you buy at the shop that is packed loosely or in bags?
What do you buy at the shop that is packed tightly together?

How long? How high?

Work in groups of three. Choose how you want to move. Before you move take turns to estimate how far you will go.

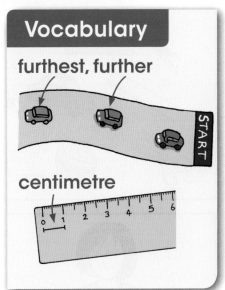

How close was your estimate?

Decide how you want to record what you did.

Can you find other ways of measuring length at school or at home?

What equipment will you need?

What questions will you need to ask?

How are you going to record what you have found out?

Mobiles

Can you add more objects to your mobile?

Can you add more levels to your mobile?

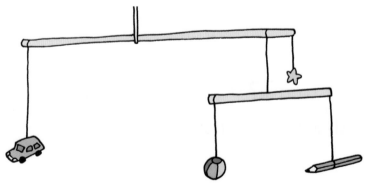

Measuring time

Jose uses a one-minute sand timer to record how long his brother can keep a football in the air.

He records his results in the table below.

Time (minutes and seconds)	A	B	C	D
	1 minute	30 seconds	2 minutes	?

How long was the last measurement? How do you know?

How many seconds is shown on each stopwatch?

How could you use this analogue stopwatch to record a time of over 60 seconds?

How long did it take Michael to walk around the classroom three times?

Who's the winner?

Ajit threw a beanbag 5 paces.
Mohinder threw a beanbag 18 paces.
Sewa threw a beanbag 11 paces.

Who was the winner? How do you know?

Dinesh ran the race in 12 seconds.
Gopal ran the race in 22 seconds.
Vishni ran the race in 17 seconds.

Who was the winner? How do you know?

Does the winner always have the shortest time?
With some friends, try the races yourself.
Who do you think will win?

How high can you jump?

How high do you think you can jump if you change the way you start?

Try different ways of jumping.

You could bend your knees and push on your feet.

You could swing your arms up as you jump.

Or choose a different way of your own.

Which was the best way to start a jump?
Did the tallest learners jump the highest?
Collect information about the jumps in your class.
Who managed to jump the highest?

Baking biscuits

200 grams of flour:

100 grams of margarine:

Gingerbread

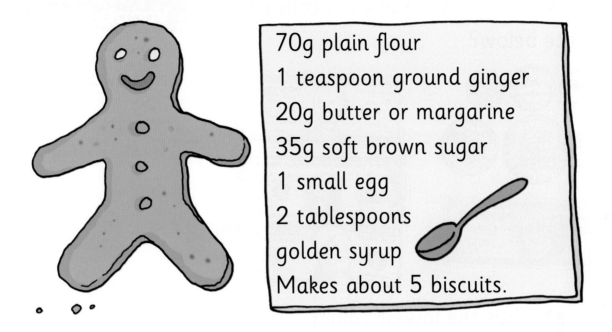

70g plain flour

1 teaspoon ground ginger

20g butter or margarine

35g soft brown sugar

1 small egg

2 tablespoons golden syrup

Makes about 5 biscuits.

What if you want to make ten biscuits?

How much of the following ingredients would you need:

- Flour?
- Ginger?
- Butter?
- Sugar?
- Eggs?
- Golden syrup?

What if you wanted to make enough biscuits for all of your class?
You need to think about how many learners there are and how
you could change the weight or quantity of the ingredients in
the recipe.

How much?

Do you know the value of each coin and banknote below?

Vocabulary

currency: the money used by a country.

Which coin has the lowest value?

Which coin has the highest value?

How many quarters are there in one dollar?

Which banknote has the highest value?

If I use a $10 bill to pay for something that costs $7, how much change would I get?

If an ice cream costs two dollars, and I get three dollars change, what banknote did I use?

If I wanted to buy a sandwich, a drink of water and a banana, how much would it cost me?

What money could I give the seller?

Tens and more

How many different two-digit and three-digit numbers can you make with these cards?

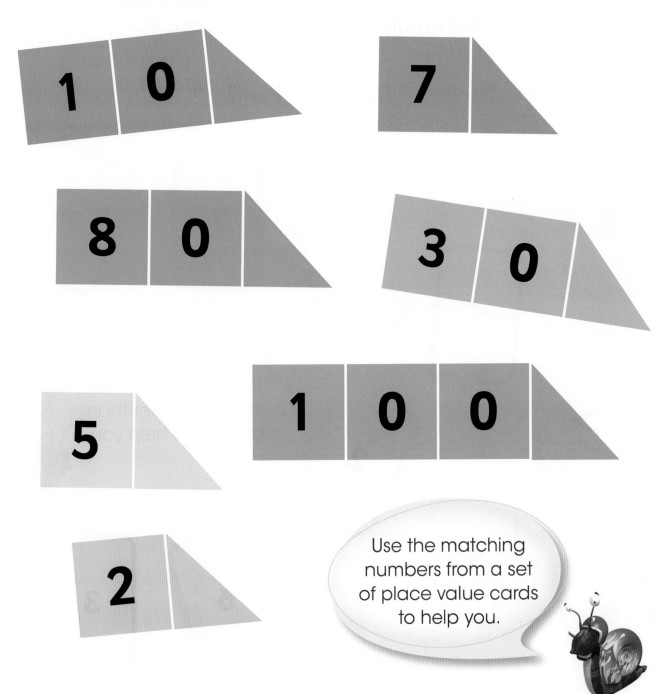

Use the matching numbers from a set of place value cards to help you.

Put your numbers in order, from the smallest to the largest.

How many tens are there in each of your numbers?

Greater than, less than

Sumi used all the digit cards below to make some number sentences.
But the cards were blown off the table!

What could her number sentences have been?

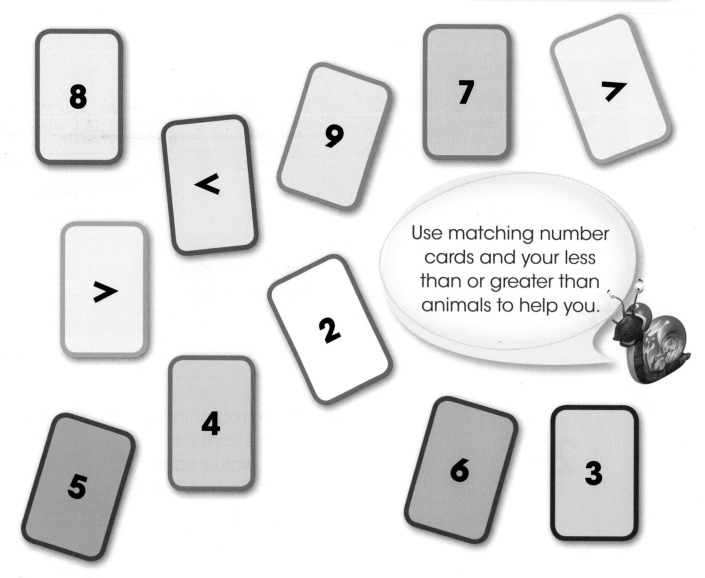

Use matching number cards and your less than or greater than animals to help you.

Remember to use **all** the cards, especially the < and >.

How many different sets of number sentences can you find?

Estimating

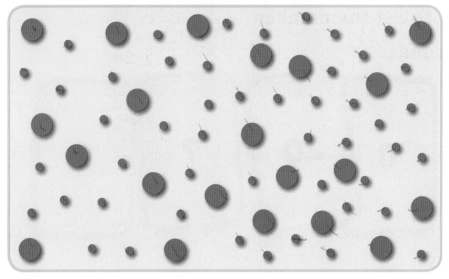

Estimate how many large dots there are.
Estimate how many small dots there are.

Place a grain of rice on each large dot; then count the grains of the rice to find out how many large dots there are.

Group your rice into twos, fives or tens to help you find out how many.

Do the same for the small dots.

Were your estimates close to the actual count?

Look around the classroom.
Choose a collection of items (pencils, scissors, rubbers or something else).
Estimate how many there are and then count them.
Were your estimates close?

Pairs to twenty

Challenge your partner to list the number
pairs to 20 in thirty seconds.

What pairs did they miss?

Now you try. Did you miss any pairs?

Repeat this activity until both you and your partner can recall
all the number pairs to 20 in thirty seconds.

Now work with a different partner.

Say a number from 1 to 20.
Your partner has to call out the other number
in the number pair to 20 as quickly as possible.

Swap over roles so that your partner calls out a
number from 1 to 20 and you say the number pair.

Double lines

Mark some numbers on your copy of each number line below.

Write the double of that number above the number line.

What is the largest number you can double?

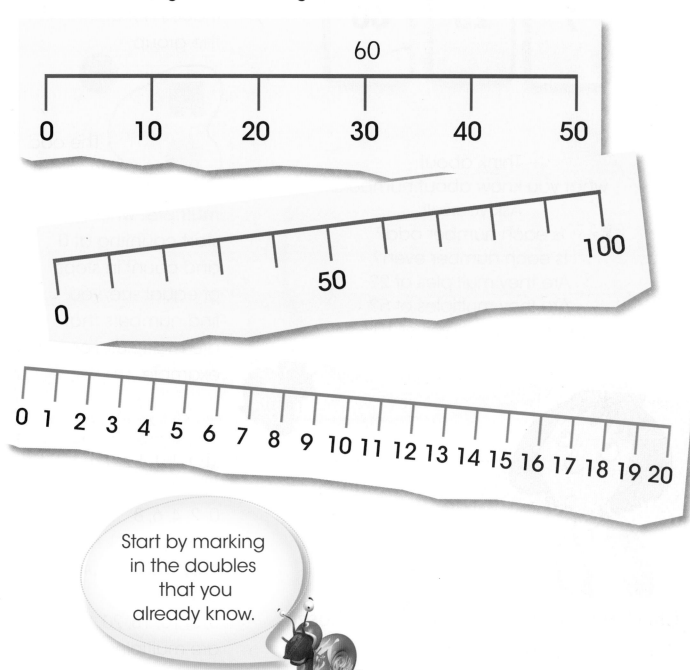

Start by marking in the doubles that you already know.

Can you double some numbers that are not on your number line?

Odd one out

Which number could be the odd one out?

7   **25**   **60**

Why?

Think about
what you know about numbers.
Ask yourself:
Is each number odd?
Is each number even?
Are they multiples of 2?
Are they multiples of 5?
Are they multiples of 10?
Or something else?

Check with a partner. Have they chosen the same number?

What reason did they have?

How many different reasons can you think of for each number to be the odd one out?

Vocabulary

odd one out: different to all others; it does not belong in the group.

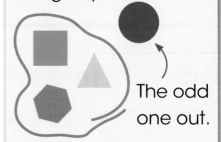

The odd one out.

multiple: when you start counting at 0 and count in steps of equal size, you find numbers that are multiples. For example,

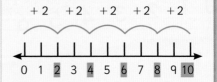

0, 2, 4, 6, 8 … increase by steps of 2, and they are multiples of 2.

0, 5, 10, 15, 20, 25… are multiples of 5.

Number stories

Make up a story to go with one of these number sentences.

$12 + 6 = 18$

$24 - 9 = 15$

$18 - 6 = 12$

$46 + 7 = 53$

$15 + 9 = 24$

$53 - 7 = 46$

Think about how you will use the numbers in the number sentence in your story.

Tell your story to a partner.
Can they tell you which number sentence you used?

Work with a partner.
Choose a number sentence and tell a story.
Your partner then tells a story to undo your number sentence.
For example, if the story is about $15 + 9 = 24$, the undoing story would be about $24 - 9 = 15$.

Addition loop

Here are two cards from an addition loop game.
The game is for two children and has eight cards altogether.

I am 34
Who is
25 + 2?

I am 27
Who is
14 + 8?

All eight cards can be arranged into a loop. To make a loop you need to match the bottom of one card to the correct answer at the top of a **different** card. The two cards above can be matched like this.

I am | 34 | Who is | 25 + 2?

I am | 27 | Who is | 14 + 8?

25 + 2 = 27

Make the other six cards for the game.

Play the game with a partner.
Does the game work wherever you start?
If not, which numbers need to be changed to make it work?

Find the difference

Find the difference between each set of objects below.
Write the matching number sentence.

Vocabulary

difference: how many more is needed to make the smaller amount the same as the larger amount.
For example:

6 − 4 = 2.
The difference between 6 and 4 is 2.

A

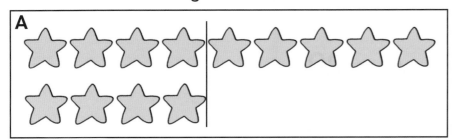

B

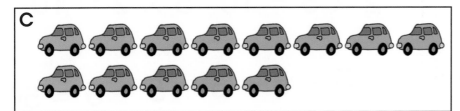

C

D

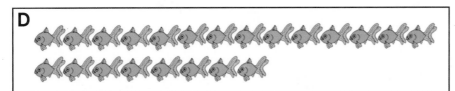

E

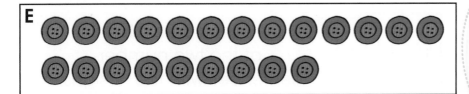

Use a straight edge to make a line at the end of the smaller row. Then count how many objects come after the line in the longer row.

Draw two different pictures to show a difference of four.

Where are the arrays?

A group of children made some arrays.
Below are the labels for their arrays.

$5 + 5 + 5 + 5 = 20$

$4 + 4 + 4 + 4 + 4 = 20$

$4 \times 5 = 20$ $5 \times 4 = 20$

$2 + 2 + 2 + 2 + 2 = 10$

$5 + 5 = 10$

$2 \times 5 = 10$ $5 \times 2 = 10$

$5 + 5 + 5 + 5 + 5 + 5 + 5 + 5 + 5 + 5 = 50$

$10 + 10 + 10 + 10 + 10 = 50$

$10 \times 5 = 50$ $5 \times 10 = 50$

Draw an array to match each label.

Now draw an array for 15.

How many in each column?

How many in each row?

Look carefully at the two number sentences with the '+' signs, to find out how many in each row and column.

Shoe boxes

These boxes of shoes have just been delivered to the shoe shop.
There is a pair of shoes in each box.

How many shoes are there in total?

Count in twos to find
how many shoes
in each column of
boxes. Then count the
number of columns.

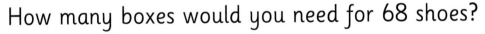

How many boxes would you need for 68 shoes?
Draw some shoe boxes.
Challenge your partner to work out how many shoes there are.

Hands up!

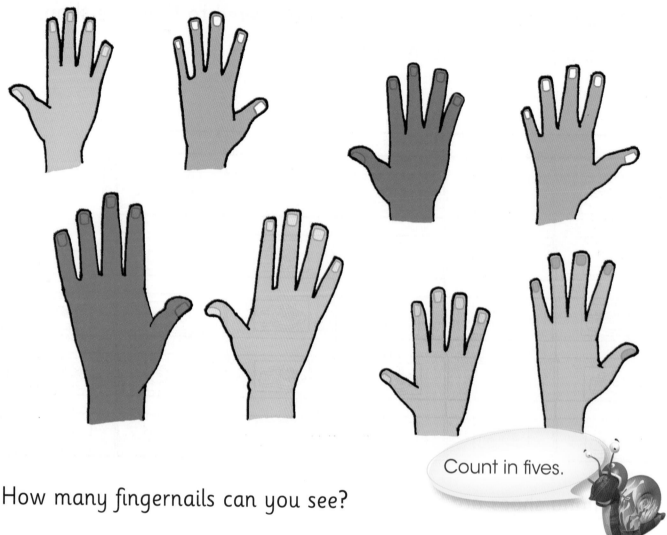

Count in fives.

How many fingernails can you see?

How many hands would you need for there to be 60 fingernails?

What if there were 60 fingernails **and** toenails **in total**?
How many people would there be?

How many fingernails are there in your classroom today?
How could you find out?
How could you work out how many fingernails there are in the whole school today?

Biscuits

Write a number sentence using division for what you can see in the picture.

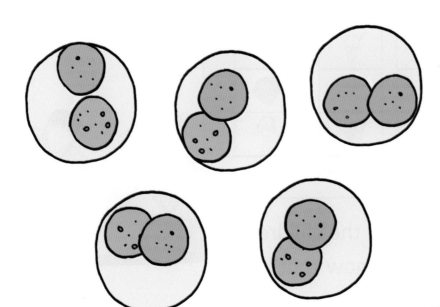

Vocabulary

division: sorts objects into smaller amounts by grouping them. For example, 12 cubes arranged in groups of 4 gives 3 groups.

$12 \div 4 = 3$

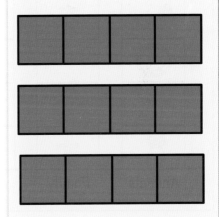

How many biscuits were there before they were put into groups of 2?

What if there had been 15 biscuits in the packet?

Draw a picture and write the number sentence to go with it.

Block graphs

Look at the block graph below.

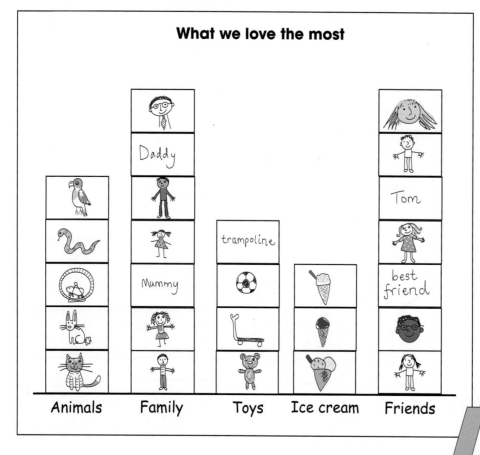

How many different things do the children love the most? How did you know that?

Which thing do most children love the most?
Which thing do least children love the most?

Make up some questions to ask your partner about the block graph.

What other questions can you ask your friends so that you can make a different block graph?

Comparing data

This is a block graph drawn by class A.

What information does it show?

What questions do you think were asked?
Think of three questions to ask a partner about class A's graph.

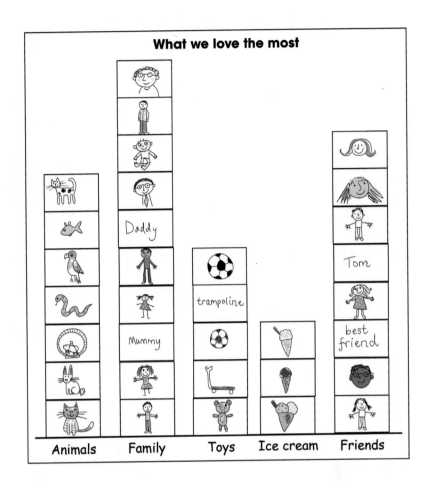

This is a block graph drawn by class B.

What information does it show?
What questions do you think were asked?
Think of three questions to ask a partner about this graph.

What I love the most

Use the data that you collected about what your group loves the most.

Draw or write what they love.

Copy the Venn diagram below. Sort your data and add labels.

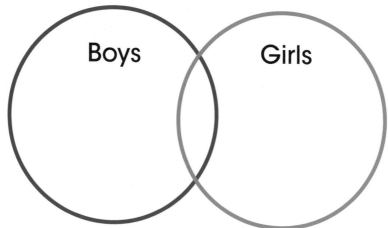

Boys   Girls

Make a block graph for the same data.

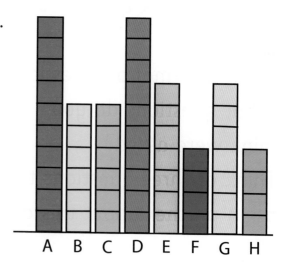

Which do you think is the best way to show the data? Why?
Share your thoughts with your group.
Do you all agree?

Think of some other questions you could ask.

Nesting Shapes

nesting objects:

If you made a set of nesting cubes would you make each one in the same way, or in a different way? Why?

How could you test that your shapes will fit inside each other?

What would be the most shapes you could make that fitted inside each other?

Paper aeroplanes

Aziz's plane flew 1 metre.

Nasreen's plane flew 3 metres.

Khalid's plane flew 50 cm.

Which plane flew the furthest distance?

They threw their planes again.

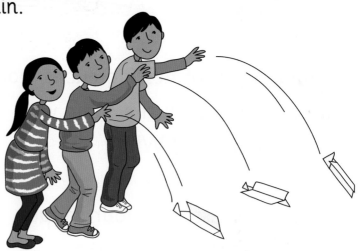

Nasreen's plane flew half a metre.

Aziz's plane flew 1 and a half metres.

Khalid's plane flew 2 metres.

Which plane flew the furthest this time?

What is the total distance travelled by each plane?

Add up their distance from both flights to find out.

Which plane flew the furthest in total?

Which plane would you use to compete in a distance race? Why?

Making puppets

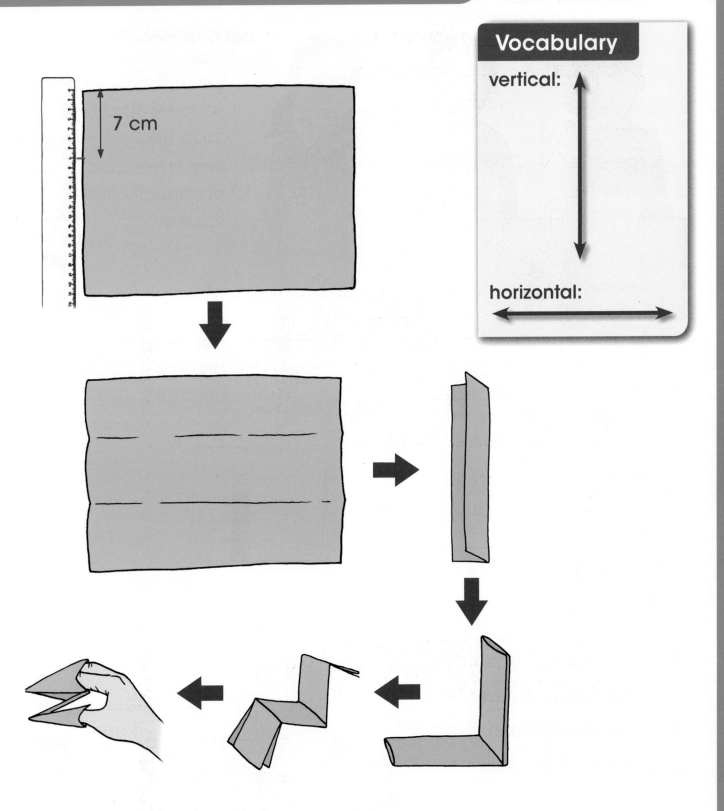

7 cm

Jugs

Vocabulary

volume: how much space a 3D object takes up.

litre: a measure of capacity and volume.

capacity: the amount a 3D object can hold.

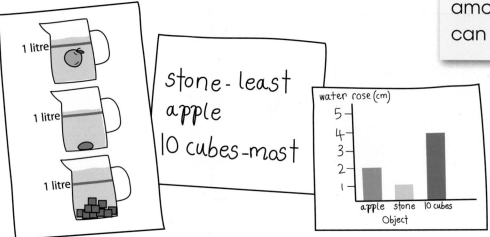

stone - least
apple
10 cubes - most

What would happen if you changed the container? What would happen if you changed the objects you used?

Making a litre

Each jug contains 1 litre of water. The bucket contains more than 1 litre. The glass contains less than 1 litre.

jug

glass

bucket

What would happen if each learner poured their water into the green container below?

Would there be too much water?
Would there be not enough water?
Would the water be just right?
How do you know?

What would happen if you changed the shape or size of the container?

What would happen if you changed the amount of water?

Think of some other questions to ask your friends.

Fill the bucket

Seymor and Judith want to calculate the capacity of their identical buckets.

Seymor uses a 1 litre jug to pour water into his bucket.

Judith uses a half-litre jug to pour water into her bucket.

Seymor needed 4 jugs of water to fill his bucket.

Judith needed 8 jugs of water to fill her bucket.

What if Seymor uses the smaller jug? What would his label say?
What if Judith uses the larger jug, what would her label say?
How do you know?

Is there a way that each learner could use both jugs to fill their buckets?
How many different ways could they do that?
Example: 2 big jugs (2 × 1 litres) and 4 small jugs (4 × half-litre.)
Find as many different ways as you can.

Number balance

This is a number balance.
It uses weights.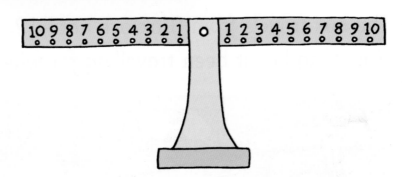

The weights can be hung on number hooks.
Equal numbers balance.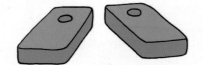

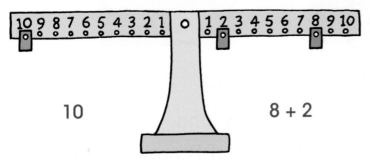

10   8 + 2

Imagine that you hang a weight on the number 9.
Where will two other weights go on the other side to make it
balance? Is there only one way? Find as many different ways
as you can.

Imagine that you hang two weights on the number 10 on one
side. How many weights would you need to make it balance
if you used just the number 5 hook on the other side?
Investigate using hooks other than number 5.

Choose another number to investigate.
Estimate where you will need to put the weights to make it
balance. Set a similar challenge for a partner.

Time travel

The bus travels from 9 o'clock until 12 o'clock.
How long has it been travelling for when it stops?

Sid has a town play mat. Road A is 10 cm long.
Road B is 1 metre long and Road C is 15 cm long.
He moves his toy car along road A, then Road B and stops at the
end of Road C.
How far has Sid's toy car travelled in total?

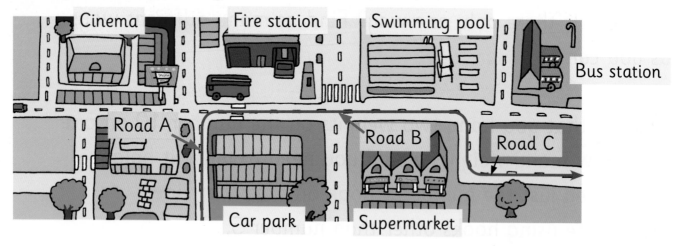

Can you make up your own story about a journey?
It should include adding together different distances,
or measuring time.
Share your story with a partner and ask them questions.

Moving time

Look at the way these learners are moving.

How are you going to move?

What if you changed the distance?

What difference would that make?

Make the distance longer or shorter and do the activity again.

What did you find out?

Which double?

A group of learners made the numbers below using a set of place value cards.

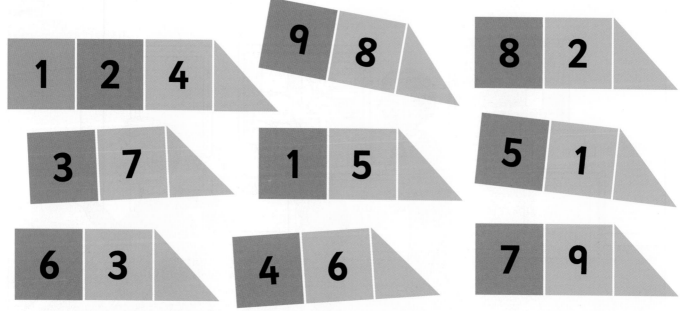

Then they doubled each number.

102   126   164   92   158

248

74   196   30

> Work out each double first, and then match them to the written numbers.

Match each double to one of the numbers made using the place value cards.

Use a set of place value cards to make your own numbers.
Then double them.
Make sure you know which double belongs to each number.

Planet Tribly

Triblets live on the planet Tribly. They have one head
but they have three eyes!

> In fact, they also have …
>
> 3 ears!
>
> 3 arms!
>
> 3 legs!
>
> 3 toes on each foot!
>
> 3 fingers on each hand!

You are an astronaut who has landed on the planet Tribly.
Triblets are shy, so they are peeking out from behind a wall.

How many Triblets are there?

How many legs are hidden behind the wall?

How many toes?

On another day, there are 21 legs behind the wall.

How many toes are there? How many Triblets are there?

Triblets have pets called tripods. They also have three of everything.

Draw a pet tripod.

Remember
to count in
threes.

Planet Quadling

Planet Quadling is next door to planet Tribly.
Quadlets look like Triblets but they have four of nearly everything.

A group of Quadlets have each brought
a friend from Tribly to see a show.
There are 28 legs altogether.
How many Quadlets are there?

How many legs will there be when
there are ten Quadlets each with a
friend from Tribly?

Think carefully.
When do you need
to count in threes?
When do you
need to count
in fours?

Odd?

Use the words and symbols in the grid to make three sentences.

You can use each word and symbol only once. Each sentence needs three words and two symbols. Each sentence must be true.

odd	even	=
odd	even	=
odd	even	=
odd	even	+
+	even	+

Vocabulary

consecutive (next door numbers): are next to each other; each number is one more than the one before.

+ 1   + 1   + 1   + 1   + 1

1   2   3   4   5   6

There is a pattern in next door numbers of odd-even-odd-even-odd-even. Use this pattern to help you.

Use some real numbers to check your sentences are true.

How do you know your sentences are correct?

What goes where?

Write some number sentences using only these numbers.
You can only use a number once.
Can you use all the numbers?

Start by writing a number sentence with missing numbers. Then, fill in the blanks one at a time.

20
13
18
50
7
125
80
36
9
150
27
12
24
75
70

Compare your number sentences with a partner.
Did they write the same ones?

Add or subtract?

Decide if you need to add or subtract for each question below.
Write the matching number sentence, then find the answers.

There are 120 bananas in a box.
At the end of the week, 6 are left.
How many were eaten?

Look for clues!
For example, 'more' usually means 'add', and 'left' usually means 'take away'.

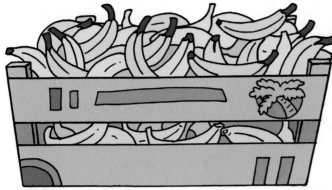

I collect stickers. I had 63 yesterday.
Today I got 8 more.
How many do I have now?

Write a number story for each
of these number sentences.
240 − 8 = 232
175 + 6 = 181

Fraction parts

Vocabulary

quarter ($\frac{1}{4}$): one of four pieces of equal size.

three-quarters ($\frac{3}{4}$): three of four pieces of equal size.

There are 12 socks.

Draw half of the socks. Label your picture $\frac{1}{2}$.

Draw and label a quarter and three-quarters of the socks.

What if you had 20 socks?

Can you work out what $\frac{1}{4}$, $\frac{1}{2}$ and $\frac{3}{4}$ of 20 is?

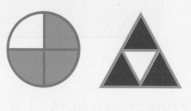

Use 20 cubes as socks to help you.

Marching ants

How many marching ants are there?

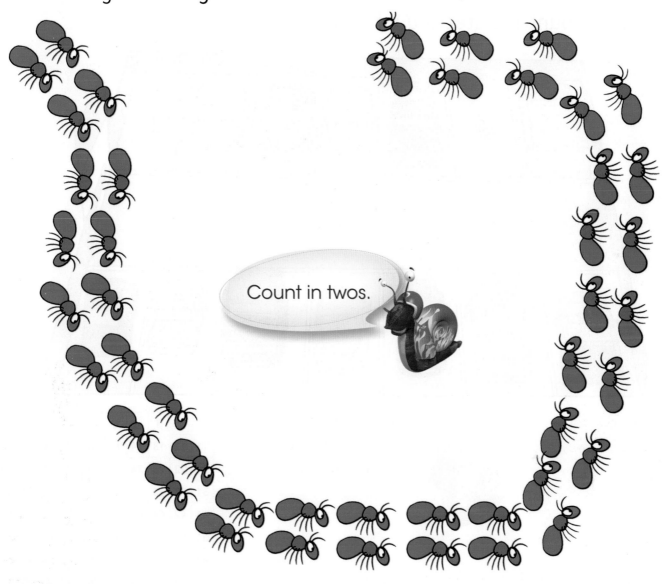

Count in twos.

Choose an even number of ants.

Draw them marching in twos.

Challenge a partner to count how many ants you have drawn.

They should count in twos.

What might happen if there were an odd number of ants?

Car park

How many wheeels are there in the car park?

Do **not** count the steering wheels.

Use a 100 square to help you count in fours.

1	2	3	4	5	6	7	8	9	10
11	12	13	14	15	16	17	18	19	20
21	22	23	24	25	26	27	28	29	30
31	32	33	34	35	36	37	38	39	40
41	42	43	44	45	46	47	48	49	50
51	52	53	54	55	56	57	58	59	60
61	62	63	64	65	66	67	68	69	70
71	72	73	74	75	76	77	78	79	80
81	82	83	84	85	86	87	88	89	90
91	92	93	94	95	96	97	98	99	100

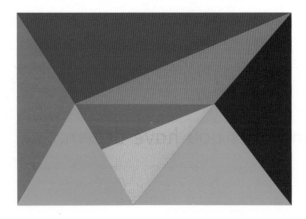

Make a pattern with lots of triangles.

How many corners are there?

Count in threes to find out.

Cake tray

Can you see cakes in groups of ten?
What about groups of four?

How many cakes in each row? How many cakes in each column?

Draw a loop around each group of ten on your worksheet.
Draw a loop around each group of four.

How many cakes are there in total?
Write some number sentences about the cakes using
the $\times$ or $\div$ sign.

Can you find another way to arrange the cakes on the tray?
Draw round each group.
Write some matching number sentences for your arrangement.

What if there had been 36 cakes?
How could they be arranged on the tray?
Draw your arrangements and write some number sentences
about them.

Sentence sort

Arrange the cards below into three correct number sentences.

Work out the answer to each calculation first. Then find the two cards with the same total.

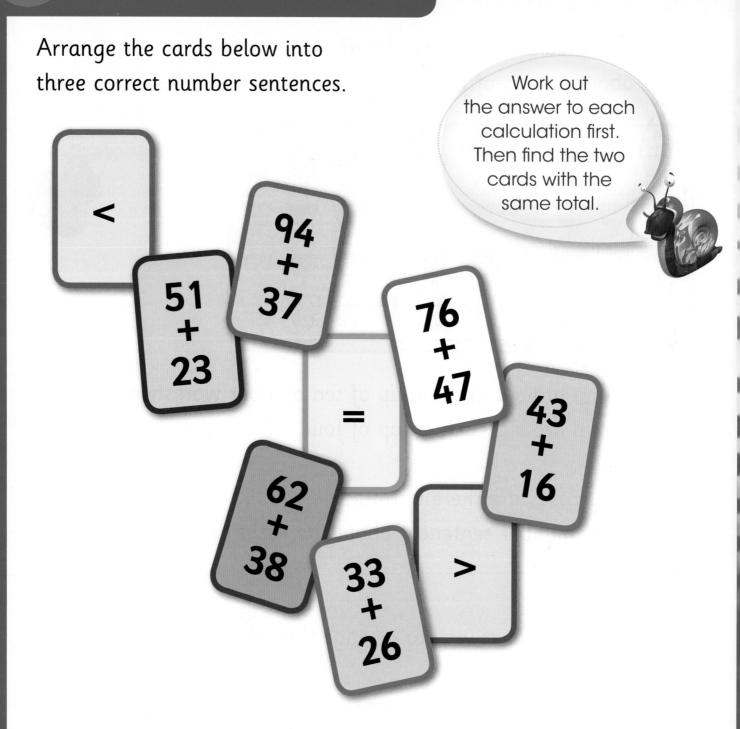

< 51 + 23 94 + 37 = 76 + 47 43 + 16 62 + 38 33 + 26 >

Compare your number sentences with a partner.

Have you made the same number sentences?

Are both sets of sentences correct?

Shapes (1)

Use some shapes. What can you find out?

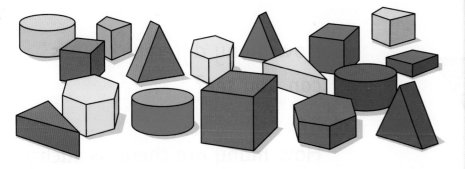

Can you:

Find different ways to make a 6-sided shape?

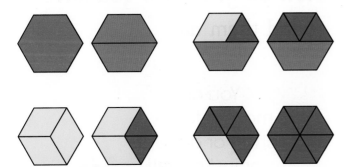

Find different ways to make a 5-sided shape?

Find different ways to make an 8-sided shape?

Make different shapes with just two shapes.
How many different ones can you make?

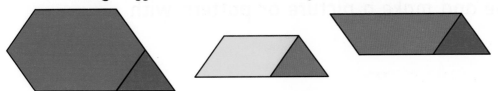

What if you join your set of shapes with your partner's set of shapes? What shapes can you make now?

Vocabulary

pentagon: a shape with 5 sides.

hexagon: a shape with 6 sides.

octagon: a shape with 8 sides.

Shapes (2)

This robot is made up from lots of 2D shapes.

How many different shapes can you see?

How many are there of each shape?

How do you know you have found them all?

You can make a table, a chart or a graph or just count!

Make other 2D shape pictures of your own.

What pictures could you make if you used just circles?

Choose any shape and make a picture or pattern with just that shape.

Can you make a picture with your partner using just three shapes? How many different shapes could you make using four shapes?

Unit 3B Core activity 28.2 7-piece tangam

Dance directions

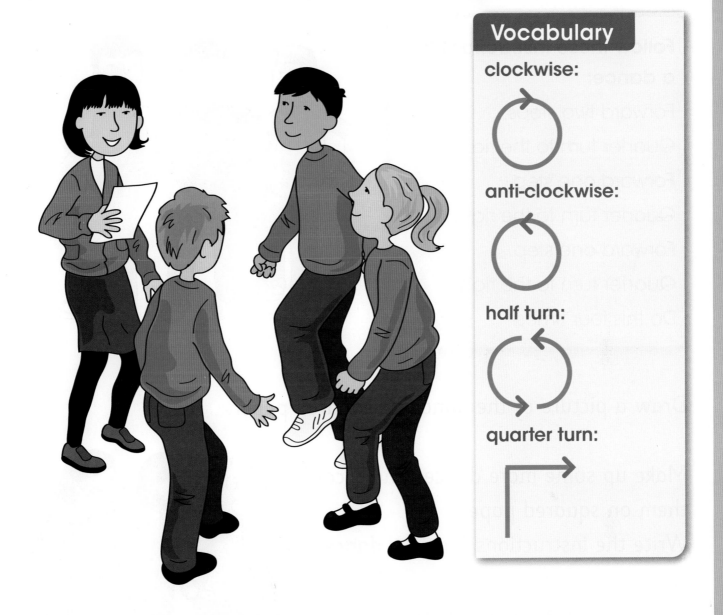

Vocabulary

clockwise:

anti-clockwise:

half turn:

quarter turn:

What if you made or found some music for your dance?

What if the whole class did your dance all at the same time?

More dancing

Follow these instructions for a dance:

Forward two steps.

Quarter turn to the right.

Forward one step.

Quarter turn to the right.

Forward one step.

Quarter turn to the right.

Do this four times.

Draw a picture of the dance on squared paper.

Make up some more dances and record them on squared paper.
Write the instructions for your dance.

Can you make a dance pattern that has a square hole in the middle?
What different dance patterns can you make?

Using a mirror

Can you draw half a picture?

Give it to a partner. Can they guess what the picture is?
Check using a mirror.

Patchwork

Look at the pictures.

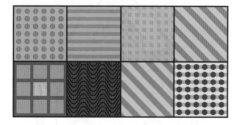 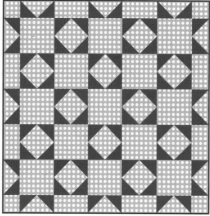 

What can you see?
Talk about what you can see.

What other patterns can you
make using squares and triangles
with a right angle?
What if all of the triangles are
not the same size?

Balls

Look at the block graph.

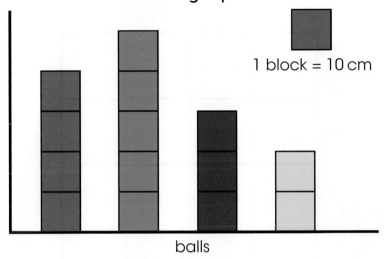

1 block = 10 cm

balls

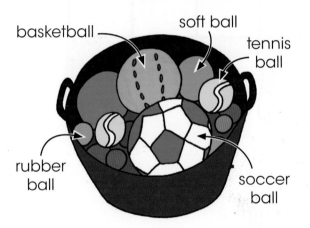

basketball

soft ball

tennis ball

rubber ball

soccer ball

Which type of ball do you think is shown by the red bar? Why?
What about the other colours?
Which ball bounces the highest and which ball bounces the least?

What if you had a super ball that could bounce the same as all of the heights added together?
How high would that bounce be?

What if you used only big balls?
Would they always bounce to the same height as each other?
What if you used only small balls?
Would they bounce to the same height as each other?
How do you know?
Why do some balls bounce higher than others?

Games

You will need:

A coin to flip.

A pile of 32 coins.

Flip the coin.

If the coin lands on a 'head' choose one coin.

If it's tails choose two coins.

Put the coins on your grid, one coin to a square.

When all of the squares are filled, count how much money you have in total.

Is this a good game?

How could you make it better?

How could you make your game harder?

How could you make your game easier?

Time tockers

Here is a tocker.  You will need:

a round lid and some plasticine.

Try different ways of putting the plasticine in the base of the lid.
What difference does it make to how the tocker rocks?

Use more or less plasticine. What difference does that make to
how the tocker rocks?

Which tocker rocked for longer?
How do you know?   Which stopped first?   Which stopped last?

What if you used lids of different sizes?
What do you think would happen?

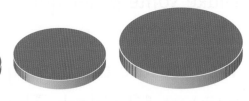

Use one of the tockers.
How high can you build a tower before the tocker stops rocking?
How many pegs can you put in a pegboard before the tocker
stops rocking?
Make up some challenges for your friends.

Time travelling

You have lots of friends all over the world.

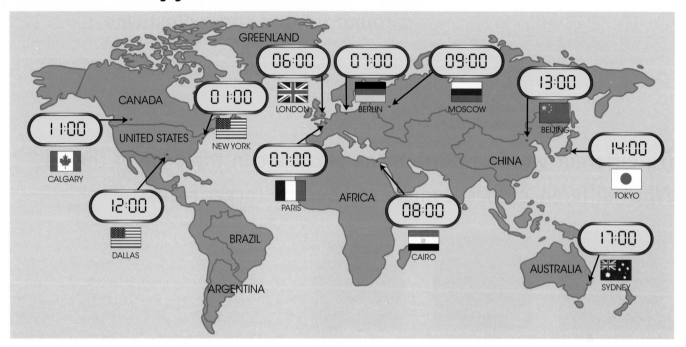

If you were having breakfast at 8am in Tokyo ● what would your friend in Sydney ✶ be doing?

If you were having lunch at 1pm in Paris ▮ what would your friend in New York ▤ be doing?

If you were asleep at 10pm in Cairo ▬ what would your friend in Belgium ▮ be doing?

Make some other questions to ask your partner.

We measure the day by saying that the sun is at its highest point at 12 o'clock. This is also called noon. The earth spins as it travels around the sun.

So if it is noon where you are, does this mean that it is dark on the opposite side of the world? Will this always be true?

Make up a story

What do you know about money?

When do you use it?

Use the money that you know to make up a story.

It can be a shopping story or a pocket money story.

Or something else.

Talk to your partner.

What if you put all of your money stories in a book with everyone else's stories, how many would there be?

You could all share your stories with the whole of the class.

Treasure trove

You will need: A 1–6 dice, a counter each, a set of pirate cards and a partner to play the game with you.

Start on the pirate, then take turns to throw the dice and move that number of spaces.

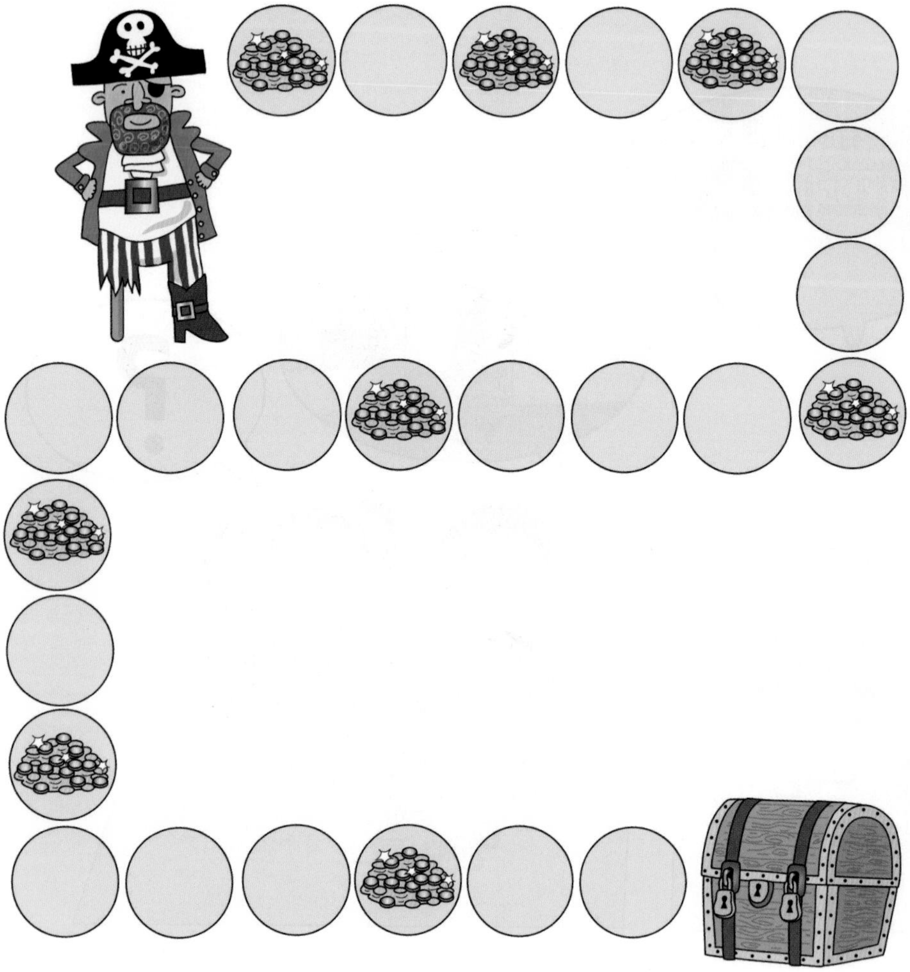

How to play

1. When you land on a 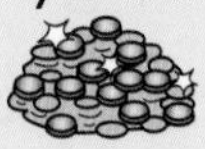 choose a card.
2. Add the amounts on the card. How much money do you have?
3. Ask your partner to check your answer.
   If you are correct, move your counter to the next space. Keep the card.
   If you are not correct, put the card back at the bottom of the pile.
4. When you get to the treasure chest, total all of your money.
5. The winner is the player with the highest total.

Is this a good or bad game?

What made it a good or bad game?

Talk with your partner and make better rules for the game.

How would you change it?

When it is changed, play it.